★★
★The Library of
American Landmarks™

MOUNT RUSHMORE

Thomas S. Owens

The Rosen Publishing Group's
PowerKids Press™
New York

Published in 1997 by The Rosen Publishing Group, Inc.
29 East 21st Street, New York, NY 10010

First Edition

Book Design: Danielle Primiceri

Photo Credits: Cover © Dick Dietrich/FPG International; pp. 4–5, 12 © Miwako Ikeda/International Stock; p. 7 © Larry Atoppy/FPG International; p. 8 © FPG International; p. 11 © Telegraph Color Library/FPG International; p. 11 (inset) Photoworld/FPG International; p. 14 © R. S. Holmberg/FPG International; p. 18 © Bettmann; p. 20 © Peter Gridley/FPG International.

Owens, Tom, 1960–
    Mount Rushmore / Thomas S. Owens.
        p.   cm. — (The Library of American landmarks)
    Includes index.
    Summary: Relates the conception and execution of the giant monument to four American presidents carved upon Mount Rushmore.
    ISBN 0-8239-5017-4
    1. Mount Rushmore national Memorial (S.D.)—Juvenile literature. [1. Mount Rushmore National Memorial (S.D.) 2. National Monuments.] I. Title. II. Series.
    F657.R8094 1997
    978.3'93—dc21   97-11539
                                                                                                          CIP
                                                                                                           AC

Manufactured in the United States of America

Table of Contents

Think Big!

Doane Robinson loved stories about his state, South Dakota. In 1924, as head of the South Dakota Historical Society, he wanted people to visit the state he loved so much. He thought that a huge **sculpture** (SKULP-cher) of historic heroes might attract them. Not since the Statue of Liberty in 1886 had America built or been given a giant **monument** (MON-yoo-ment).

In Georgia, a **sculptor** (SKULP-ter) named Gutzon Borglum was carving a huge statue of a soldier on horseback. Borglum knew how to think big. Robinson knew Borglum could build the monument he wanted.

Doane Robinson wanted to create a huge monument that would draw thousands of people to South Dakota. Seventeen years later, his monument became a reality.

Why Them?

Robinson and Borglum chose Mount Rushmore in the Black Hills as the place to carve their monument. Robinson wanted the monument to feature famous Western heroes, such as explorers Lewis and Clark or Chief Red Cloud of the Sioux Indian Nation. But Borglum knew that in order to get visitors from all over the country, the monument needed **subjects** (SUB-jekts) that everyone would know. He decided to carve images of the four U.S. presidents he believed to be the best: George Washington, Thomas Jefferson, Abraham Lincoln, and Theodore Roosevelt.

Mount Rushmore, a mountain in the Black Hills of South ▶ Dakota, was a perfect place for Borglum's monument.

CANADA

MONTANA

NORTH
DAKOTA

MINNESOTA

MOUNT RUSHMORE

SOUTH
DAKOTA

WYOMING

NEBRASKA

IOWA

Big Plans

Borglum started by making a **plaster** (PLAS-ter) model of Mount Rushmore. One inch on the model was equal to one foot on the mountain. Borglum decided to carve only the heads of the presidents. Each model head was five feet tall. Each mountain head would be 60 feet tall. If Mount Rushmore's presidents had bodies to match their heads, they would each be about 465 feet tall!

◀ The plaster model that Borglum made of his monument showed the heads and chests of each president. But once Borglum started working on the mountain, he decided to carve just the heads.

Dedicated to Patriotism

In 1927, President Calvin Coolidge visited Mount Rushmore. He officially **dedicated** (DED-ih-kay-ted) the monument. "The people of the future will see history and art combined to portray the spirit of **patriotism** (PAY-tree-uh-tizm)," said President Coolidge. The U.S. Congress voted to give government money to support Borglum's work. But it wasn't enough.

President Calvin Coolidge believed that Mount Rushmore would stand for the patriotism and pride that people felt ▶ for the United States.

Words to Remember

Part of Borglum's work was making Americans believe they needed a huge monument. More than $100,000 had to be raised during the 1930s. This was during the **Depression** (dee-PRESH-un), a time when most American people had little money. Through speeches, newspaper articles, and stories, Borglum asked people to imagine the four presidents "carved high, as close to heaven as we can. Then, breathe a prayer that the wind and rain alone shall wear them away."

Borglum convinced people all across the United States to help fund his work at Mount Rushmore. ▶

Americans imagined. Even schoolchildren sent extra pennies to help Borglum create his dream for the future.

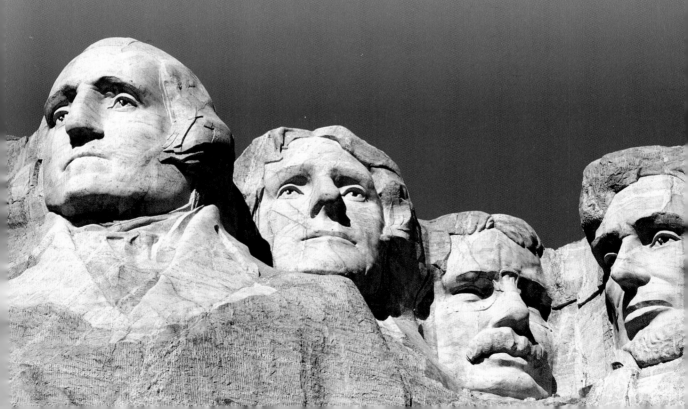

Making Mount Rushmore

Borglum couldn't create Mount Rushmore alone. **Miners** (MY-nerz), **loggers** (LOG-erz), and ranchers were among the 400 men hired to help make the monument. Because of the Depression, one in four Americans was out of work. The people of South Dakota were happy for any work they could get. The pay ranged from 50 cents up to one dollar per hour, which went to the **experienced** (ex-PEER-ee-enst) stone carvers. Each day began with a journey of three miles to the mountain, and then a climb of 760 stairs to the top of Mount Rushmore.

◀ During the fourteen years it took to finish the monument, not one worker was killed or seriously hurt.

Finishing Touches

Borglum and the workers used **dynamite** (DY-nuh-myt) and drills to remove huge chunks of rock, making the shapes of faces in the hard **granite** (GRA-nit).

Mount Rushmore could have been finished in less than seven years. But freezing weather and lack of money turned it into a fourteen-year project. In March 1941, Borglum died at the age of 73. His son, Lincoln, took over. The monument was finally finished on October 31, 1941. In the end, Mount Rushmore cost about $990,000 to build.

Experienced stone carvers worked carefully on the details of each president's face. ▶

Mount Rushmore's Match

In 1939, Sioux Chief Henry Standing Bear wrote to one of Mount Rushmore's sculptors, Casimir Ziolkowski. "My fellow chiefs and I would like the white man to know the red man has great heroes too." Seven years later, work began on another South Dakota mountain carving, the Chief Crazy Horse **Memorial** (mem-OR-ree-ul). Although Ziolkowski died in 1982, his wife and eight of his children kept working. When it is finished, their monument will be 563 feet high and 641 feet long. That's almost twice the size of the Statue of Liberty.

Chief Crazy Horse fought for the freedom and safety of the Sioux people. He is one of many ▶ Native American heroes.

Those Famous Faces

Most people around the world—even those who have never visited South Dakota—know something about Mount Rushmore. In the 1959 mystery movie *North by Northwest*, bad guys chase the two heroes around the mountain, running across the stone faces of the presidents. Cartoonists have added more famous faces, real and imaginary, to Mount Rushmore, or show the four presidents talking. Toothpaste companies have made commercials showing how Roosevelt's teeth could be brushed if he'd only smile again!

◀ People all over the world recognize the famous faces on Mount Rushmore.

Mount Rushmore Today

Today, the National Park Service takes care of Mount Rushmore. Every year, a group of workers clean and care for the faces of the four presidents. They fill cracks that form during the winter. They also make sure the whole sculpture stays strong and stable.

On July 3, 1991, there was a huge celebration for the monument's 50th anniversary. Then President George Bush and many other famous people were there in honor of this monument of four of the United States' finest leaders.

Glossary

dedicate (DED-ih-kayt) To set apart for a special reason.

Depression (dee-PRESH-un) A time during the 1930s in the United States when there was very little business and many people were out of work.

dynamite (DY-nuh-myt) A powerful explosive.

experience (ex-PEER-ee-ents) Knowing how to do something well from doing it many times.

granite (GRA-nit) A very hard, grainy rock.

logger (LOG-er) A person who cuts down trees and makes the wood ready for building.

memorial (mem-OR-ree-ul) Something that reminds people of an important person or event.

miner (MY-ner) A person who digs up minerals and special rocks.

monument (MON-yoo-ment) Something that is built to honor an important person or event.

patriotism (PAY-tree-uh-tizm) The love and pride a person has for his or her country.

plaster (PLAS-ter) A soft mixture of lime, sand, and water that hardens as it dries.

sculptor (SKULP-ter) A person who shapes stone by chipping and cutting.

sculpture (SKULP-cher) A carved figure.

subject (SUB-jekt) The person or thing an artist shows in a work of art.

Index